# DRAGONFLIES

## CATCHING · IDENTIFYING · HOW AND WHERE THEY LIVE

## CHRIS EARLEY

WITH

RHIANNON LOHR, CAMERON LOHR AND NATHAN EARLEY

FIREFLY BOOKS

# A FIREFLY BOOK

Published by Firefly Books Ltd. 2013

The publisher gratefully acknowledges the financial support for our publishing program by the Government of Canada through the Canada Book Fund as administered by the Department of Canadian Heritage

First printing

**Publisher Cataloging-in-Publication Data (U.S.)**

Earley, Chris.
 Dragonflies : catching, identifying, how and where they live / Chris Earley.
[32] p. :  col. photos. ;  cm.
Summary:  Tips and tricks on how to catch, identify and study dragonflies
ISBN-13: 978-1-77085-185-6
ISBN-13: 978-1-77085-186-3  (pbk.)
1. Dragonflies — Juvenile literature.  I. Title.
595.733  dc23    QL520.E374 2013

**Library and Archives Canada Cataloguing in Publication**

Earley, Chris G., 1968–
 Dragonflies : catching, identifying, how and where they live / Chris Earley.
ISBN 978-1-77085-185-6 (bound).
ISBN 978-1-77085-186-3 (pbk.)
 1. Dragonflies—Juvenile literature.  2. Dragonflies—Identification—Juvenile literature.  I. Title.
QL520.E27 2013      j595.7'33      C2012-906743-1

Published in the United States by
Firefly Books (U.S.) Inc.
P.O. Box 1338, Ellicott Station
Buffalo, New York 14205

Published in Canada by
Firefly Books Ltd.
50 Staples Avenue, Unit 1
Richmond Hill, Ontario L4B 0A7

Design: Erin R. Holmes/Soplari Design

Printed in China

## Dedication

To Ron, the best friend/father/uncle and dragonflying partner we could ask for!

~Chris, Rhiannon, Cameron and Nathan

## Acknowledgments

We want to thank Carl Rothfels, Colin Jones, Gord Lewer and Ed Poropat for putting up with us on all those Odonate Surveys. We also appreciate the photo contributions from Robert McCaw, Stephen Marshall, Ron Lohr and Lyndsay Fraser. Thanks also to Christen Thomas and Michael Worek, our fine editors, and to Erin Holmes for her wonderful book design.

Photo Credits: All images © Chris Earley, with the exception of the following. Page 4: (top) © Ron Lohr, (middle) © Lindsay Fraser; page 6: (top right) © Stephen Marshall, page 8: (Great crested Flycatcher) © Robert McCaw; page 9: (bottom left) © Rhiannon Lohr; page 10: (top left) © Lyndsay Fraser, (anatomy image) ©Shutterstock.com/ Le Do; page 14: (top) © Ron Lohr

# Contents

# What Is a Dragonfly?

Dragonflies are amazing insects that have long bodies and move at fast speeds. The Wandering Glider (also called the Globe Skimmer) can be found on every continent except Antarctica! One population does the longest migration of any insect. In four generations, they fly from East Africa to India and back. That's at least 14,000 miles (22,500 kilometers)!

Dragonflies come in all different shapes and sizes. Their closest relative is called a damselfly. Dragonflies and damselflies make up a group of insects called odonates. Dragonflies have been around for at least 300 million years, appearing before the dinosaurs. There are fossils of dragonflies that have a wingspan of almost 2½ feet (75 centimeters)! That's as big as a Mallard duck!

It is easy to tell dragonflies from damselflies because damselflies tend to be a lot skinnier and smaller than most dragonflies. Also, dragonflies hold their wings out beside their body, while damselflies hold their wings together and above their body. Although these insects have a lot in common, we will concentrate on dragonflies in this book.

This dragonfly is called a Chalk-fronted Corporal. It holds its wings out like other dragonflies.

This bluet damselfly holds its wings over its back like most damselflies do.

This spreadwing damselfly partially spreads its wings out when it perches.

Bogs are interesting wetlands. Some rare dragonflies only live in bogs. If you catch an Ebony Boghaunter, you know that there is likely a bog nearby.

## What Dragonflies Tell Us

Some dragonflies are very choosy about where they live. For example, some clubtails will only live in very clean, unpolluted rivers. Some other dragonflies only breed in bogs. When you catch one of these "picky" dragonflies, you know that the area you are in is likely an important spot for local wildlife. Finding a rare dragonfly can sometimes help biologists protect a natural area from being destroyed.

## Where to Look for Dragonflies

Look for dragonflies in wetlands such as streams, rivers, lakes, ponds, marshes, bogs and swamps. They like wetlands because they spend the nymph stage of their life cycle (see page 6) underwater, and it is where they lay their eggs. But you can also find them in forests, fields and even in backyards.

You can find dragonflies from early spring to late autumn. The time of day is important when looking for dragonflies. Most dragonflies start flying once the sun has warmed the air in the late morning. While most dragonflies like to fly when it is hot and sunny, some species fly well into the evening.

Springtime Darners are one of the few darners that are out in the early spring. Most darners are around in the summer and fall.

## Life Cycle

There are three stages in the life cycle of a dragonfly: egg, nymph and adult. The length of each stage of the life cycle of a dragonfly can be different depending on the species of dragonfly. Just the nymph stage of some of the bigger dragonflies can be as long as five years!

### Egg

Have you ever seen a pair of dragonflies flying together in perfect harmony? If so, you have most likely seen the mating pattern of the dragonfly. This pattern is called "the wheel."

When they are done mating, the female lays her eggs. Some dragonflies scatter their eggs in the water, some lay them on vegetation in or by the water and others lay them in wet logs or on the shore.

## Nymph

Dragonfly eggs hatch into wingless nymphs that live underwater and breathe through gills in their abdomen. Nymphs are fierce hunters and will eat anything they can catch. They have a huge lower jaw that can quickly extend and grab their prey. Some nymphs sneak up on their prey, while others hide and then pounce when the unsuspecting prey gets close enough. Dragonfly nymphs can eat small organisms such as mosquito larvae, and some can eat bigger creatures like very small fish and tadpoles.

**Dragonfly nymphs have lower jaws that shoot out to grab prey.**

**Dragonfly nymphs are underwater predators.**

**These meadowhawks are mating and are in a position called "the wheel."**

**Meadowhawk eggs**

This clubtail dragonfly is squeezing out of the back of its nymphal skin.

## Adult

When a nymph is mature, it will emerge from its skin (called an exoskeleton) to become an adult dragonfly with wings. Most nymphs emerge at night so there is less danger of birds finding and eating them.

First the nymph crawls out of the water and waits until its exoskeleton becomes dry. The nymph then starts to expand and splits the brittle skin on the top of its body. The insect then emerges from its exoskeleton. It is now an adult dragonfly. The dragonfly then pumps out its wings so that they dry properly before the dragonfly takes its first flight. The leftover exoskeleton is called the exuvium.

Its wings are now almost fully out. The dragonfly will keep its wings folded over its back for a little while before putting them out to its sides. Once it is dry, it will take its first flight.

It is now out and is pumping up its wings. Its old skin is called an exuvium.

## What Do Dragonflies Eat?

Dragonflies are predators that eat other insects. Many dragonflies catch most of their food in the air. Some sit on a perch and then fly out and attack their prey. Some kinds of dragonflies eat butterflies and even other dragonflies.

The Dragonhunter eats large insects. This one is eating another dragonfly called a Band-winged Meadowhawk.

This male Twelve-spotted Skimmer is perched and surveying his territory for prey.

This praying mantis was big enough to grab a Lance-tipped Darner.

This bird, a Great Crested Flycatcher, has caught a dragonfly and is bringing it back to the nest to feed its young.

## What Eats Dragonflies?

Dragonflies are predators, but they are also prey. Dragonflies are eaten by many different kinds of birds as well as spiders, praying mantises, frogs and bats. When the dragonfly is a nymph and living underwater, it can be eaten by small fish and larger water insects.

## How to Catch Dragonflies

To catch dragonflies, you will need a butterfly net, which is long and shaped like a cone.

Rhiannon carefully balances on a log while reaching into her net to remove a dragonfly that she has caught.

You should hold your net like a baseball bat. When the dragonfly comes close, swing the net over it sideways. If the dragonfly went in, tilt your wrist to fold the netting over the rim so the dragonfly does not fly out of the net. You can then reach in past the fold to get the dragonfly out. Note: Always look through the netting before getting the dragonfly out just in case you caught a bee or wasp at the same time without knowing it!

Hold your net like a baseball bat when you swing to catch a dragonfly.

## How to Hold a Dragonfly

When taking the dragonfly out of the net, you must hold it gently by folding all four of its wings over its back. This does not hurt the dragonfly and lets you get a good look at it. Some dragonflies can bite (their bite feels like a small pinch) when you pick them up, but they can't bite when you hold them this way. Once you have a gentle but good grip, you can then use your free hand to look through a book to identify your catch.

Nathan shows how to hold a dragonfly. This is safe for the dragonfly and stops it from nipping.

Cameron is holding a dragonfly in one hand while he looks it up in a book.

## Letting Your Dragonfly Go

When letting your dragonfly go, place it on a branch because sometimes they need some time to rest before they take off again. Another way you can release the dragonfly is by letting it go on your finger. For fun, we often let the dragonflies go on our noses!

**We put this darner on Cameron's nose!**

**This Chalk-fronted Corporal is resting on Rhiannon's finger.**

## How to Identify Dragonflies

There are more than 300 different kinds of dragonflies in North America, and you can probably find quite a few different ones right around where you live.

### Anatomy and Field Marks

Dragonflies are insects, so they have a head, a thorax and an abdomen. These body parts can help you identify your dragonfly. Different dragonflies have different markings and can be different shapes and sizes. You can look for markings such as thorax stripes, face stripes, abdomen spots, appendage shapes and wing patterns.

MARKINGS

ANATOMY

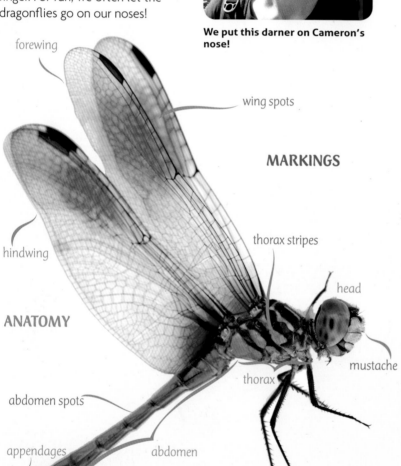

forewing

wing spots

hindwing

thorax stripes

head

mustache

thorax

abdomen spots

appendages

abdomen

**The Elfin Skimmer is one of the smallest dragonflies in the world!**

## Size

The easiest way to begin to identify dragonflies is by their size. Darners and spiketails are the largest dragonflies, and many skimmers are fairly small. The emeralds, cruisers and clubtails are generally medium-sized.

You should also try to figure out what group or family your dragonfly belongs to. The following pages show you some common dragonfly families.

**This Swamp Darner is the biggest dragonfly we have ever seen.**

**The Wandering Glider is a medium-sized dragonfly but it has very wide wings that help it travel over long distances.**

## Common Dragonfly Families

These are the kinds of dragonflies that you are most likely to find in North America.

### Darners

Darners are generally big with blue or green markings and their eyes are attached together. They often perch by hanging vertically in trees. When they are flying, they hover over land and water. Darners are common in many habitats.

### Clubtails

Clubtails range in size from small to fairly large and are generally black or brown with yellow markings. Sometimes they are green. Their eyes are separated — this is an important field mark to look for on clubtails. Clubtails often have widened clubs on the tips of their abdomens; this is how they got their name. Most perch on the ground, on rocks and on sandy paths. They are fairly common in areas with rivers, lakes and ponds.

### Spiketails

Spiketails are very big and are black with bright yellow markings. Their eyes just barely touch each other. They perch vertically, just like darners. They generally fly over marshy wetlands and aren't as common as some other dragonfly groups.

## Cruisers

Cruisers are medium to large in size and are black or brown with some light markings. They have very long legs and usually one thorax stripe. They hover over streams, lakes and marshy wetlands. Their eyes are connected, and they perch vertically.

## Emeralds

Emeralds are medium in size and very dark. They're often seen flying near coniferous forests (like pine or spruce). Many have very bright green eyes, and that is how they got their name. Their eyes are connected. They are fairly widespread.

## Skimmers

Most skimmers are small to medium in size and can be all sorts of colors. Their eyes are connected, and they perch horizontally. Some skimmers have spots on their wings and some don't. There are lots of different types of skimmers, and they can be very common.

# How You Can Help Dragonflies

A great way to be a good dragon hunter is to help out with organized dragonfly counts or surveys. On these counts, you will catch, identify and release the dragonflies. The biologists on the count will help you learn new techniques, and you might see dragonfly species that you have never seen before. Contact your local naturalist group to find out when and where the dragonfly surveys are in your area.

As you catch dragonflies, keep a record of what you have caught. If you think you have found a dragonfly that is very rare for your area, show it to a local expert by taking some pictures of it and sending them to him or her.

Once you have started dragonflying and you know your common dragonflies, you can start to introduce other kids to dragonflies, too. You can take them for a walk in a local wilderness area and teach them how to be dragon hunters!

Here we are as part of a group doing a dragonfly count. We like this photo because everyone is looking for dragonflies, but no one sees what is sitting on the one naturalist's shoulder!

This is Nathan's little sister, Skye (at age 4), with a Harlequin Darner that she caught. This was the first one recorded in the county where she found it.

One summer we found a very rare Incurvate Emerald in a spot where it has never been seen before. It has only been found in a few places in all of Ontario, Canada.

## Mini Field Guide

Here are some common dragonflies that you might come across. But remember, we are only giving a few examples here, so you may find a different species that closely matches one we show. As well, some of these may not be found where you live. You can confirm your identification with a local field guide or on the Internet (try bugguide.net). Most states and provinces have dragonfly lists that show all the species found there (try www.npwrc. usgs.gov/resource/distr/insects/dfly/index.htm).

The examples shown in this Mini Field Guide are mostly males (boys) because they are more colorful and easier to identify for beginners than the females (girls).

Watch for these clues when trying to identify dragonflies:

Size (length of their head and body together)
* very large: 2½–3½ inches (6.5–9 centimeters)
* large: ~2–2½ inches (5–6.5 centimeters)
* medium: ~1½–2 inches (4–5 centimeters)
* small: ~1½ inches (under 4 centimeters)

. Overall shape

Body coloration

. Wing patterns (spots, bands, colors)

. Flight pattern (really fast, bouncy, lots of hovering, lots of perching, flying high, skimming water surface).

# SPIKETAILS

## Twin-spotted Spiketail

* very large
* eyes touch at a point
* bright green eyes when older
* pairs of yellow abdomen spots
* two straight thorax stripes

# Darners

## Common Green Darner

- very large
- bright green thorax
- abdomen is blue in the male and reddish-brown or gray in the female

Male

Female

## Fawn Darner

- very large
- brownish overall
- two round yellow spots on the sides of the thorax

## Cyrano Darner

- very large
- two thick green stripes on the thorax
- blue "nose" that sticks out
- blue eyes
- angular shapes on the abdomen

## Swamp Darner

- very large (huge!)
- thin rings on the abdomen instead of spots
- straight, wide, green stripes on the thorax
- blue eyes

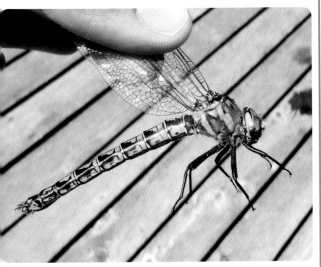

# Darners

## Lance-tipped Darner

- very large
- the first stripe on the thorax (closest to the head) is bent
- male has a small spur on his appendages

## Canada Darner

- very large
- the first stripe on the thorax is bent or notched

**Greenish Female**

## Variable Darner

- very large
- the stripes on the thorax are either very thin or broken into four spots or there is one thin stripe and two spots

## Shadow Darner

- very large
- the yellow or green stripes on the thorax have a hook shape
- male has a small spur on his appendages (like the Lance-tipped Darner has)

# CLUBTAILS

## Dragonhunter

- very large
- two thick yellow thorax stripes
- head looks small compared the to body size

## Black-shouldered Spinyleg

- large
- yellow thorax (gets greener as they get older) with thick black shoulder stripe
- long spines on hind legs

## Rusty Snaketail

- large
- wide "club" on male
- bright green thorax
- rusty brown abdomen
- pale appendages

## Unicorn Clubtail

- large
- very yellow appendages
- greenish thorax with thin dark stripes
- ridge between eyes has a small horn

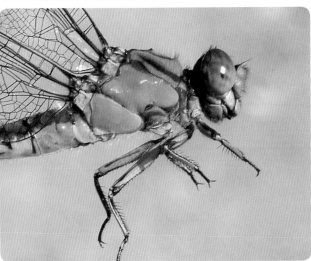

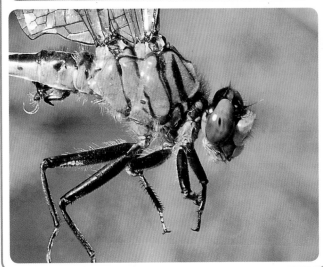

# emeralps

## American Emerald

- medium
- shiny green and bronze thorax with no yellow spots
- bright green eyes
- yellow ring at base of abdomen (near thorax)

## Clamp-tipped Emerald

- large
- shiny thorax has bright yellow spots
- long abdomen
- bright green eyes
- male's appendages look like a clamp

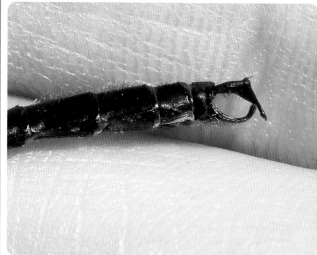

## Common Baskettail

- medium
- yellow spots along sides of the abdomen
- greenish or brownish eyes
- variable black patches on the bases of the wings

## Prince Baskettail

- very large
- variable number of wing patches at end, middle and base of wings
- long abdomen is thin where it joins the thorax

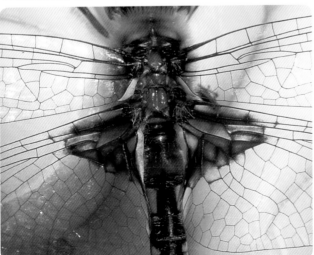

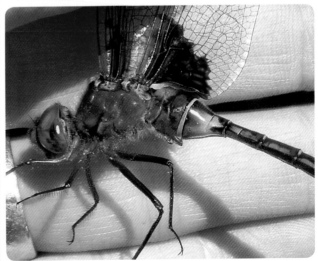

# SKIMMERS

## Twelve-spotted Skimmer

- large
- male has dark and light spots on the wings
- female and young male have straight stripes on the abdomen

## Common Whitetail

- medium
- male has whitish abdomen and wide wing patches
- female and young male have jagged stripes on the abdomen

Male

Male

Female or young male

Female

## Four-spotted Skimmer

- medium
- golden patches on the wings
- black triangles at the bases of the hind wings

## Widow Skimmer

- medium
- large black patches at bases of the wings
- adult male also has white on the wings as well
- female and young male have straight stripes on the abdomen

Male

Female or young male

# SKIMMERS

## Dot-tailed Whiteface

- small
- dot on abdomen
- white face

## Belted Whiteface

- small
- white on abdomen and may have red on thorax
- white face

## Blue Dasher

- small
- male has a blue abdomen and a green-and-black striped thorax
- female has pairs of yellow lines on abdomen
- white face

Male

Female

## Eastern Pondhawk

- medium
- male is all blue (young male may have green thorax)
- female is green with dark spots on the abdomen
- green face

Male

Female

# SKIMMERS

## Ruby, Cherry- and White-faced Meadowhawks

- small with red body, black legs, and mostly clear wings
- Ruby and Cherry-faced have a red or brown face and can be hard to tell apart
- White-faced has a white face
- Young are yellowish

young

Ruby or Cherry-faced

White-faced

## Band-winged and Autumn Meadowhawks

- small
- red body
- Band-winged with thick golden bands at bases of wings
- Autumn has mostly clear wings and yellowish-brown legs

Band-winged

Autumn

## Black Saddlebags

- large
- black patches, or "saddlebags," on the hind wings
- black abdomen with one or more pairs of yellow spots

## Wandering Glider

- large
- orange-yellow body
- fairly similar to a young meadowhawk, but much larger

# SKIMMERS

## Calico Pennant

- small
- male has red-and-black abdomen
- dark spots with red lines on the wings
- females and young males have yellow markings on the abdomen and wings instead of red

Male

Female

## Eastern Amberwing

- small
- male has golden wings
- female has brown spots on the wings
- abdomen has rings

Male

Female

# CRUISERS

## Stream Cruiser

- large
- light moustache
- one light thorax stripe
- light spots on abdomen
- very long legs

# Books about Dragonflies

*Stokes Beginner's Guide to Dragonflies*
by Blair Nikula, Jackie Sones, Donald and Lillian Stokes

This book has lots of species and goes into depth about some of their behavior. It also has very good photos and is small and portable.

*Dragonflies and Damselflies of Algonquin Provincial Park*
by Colin Jones, Andrea Kingsley, Peter Burke and Matt Holder

This is the best book for Ontario, where we live, and we use it a lot. It has a lot of information about identification, behavior, habitat and flight period. The artwork is very detailed and has good size silhouettes.

*Dragonflies of the Northwoods*
by Kurt Mead

This is a very handy book that covers many of the dragonflies found in the northern United States and Canada. There are other super insect books in this series, too.

*Dragonflies and Damselflies of the East* and *Dragonflies and Damselflies of the West*
by Dennis Paulson.

Useful books with great photos and lots of information. The two together cover all of North America.

*Dragonflies through Binoculars*
by Sidney Dunkle

This book covers all of the dragonflies in North America. It is better for information than for identification.

# Index